D1015032

Percy the Park Keeper

1·2·3

NICK BUTTERWORTH

Collins

An Imprint of HarperCollinsPublishers

First published in Great Britain by HarperCollins Publishers Ltd in 1998

This edition published in 2010

1 3 5 7 9 10 8 6 4 2

ISBN: 978-0-00-786511-6

Visit our website at: www.harpercollins.co.uk

Printed and bound in China

Hello! I'm Percy the Park Keeper.
Would you like to come and meet the
animals in my park? We will help
you to learn your numbers, and give
you some ideas for practising your
counting at home.

1 one ●

1 hut

1 mole
(and 1 hole)

1 mug

1 jug

Look in your kitchen.
Can you count 1 mug?

2   two   ●   ●

2 boots

2 slippers

2 gloves   2 socks

Look in your bedroom.
Can you count 2 socks?

3 three

3 birds

3 squirrels

3 tails

Look out of the window.
Can you count 3 birds?

4 four

4 ears   4 eyes

4 deck chairs

4 bushes

Look around the room.
Can you count 4 eyes?

5   five

5 leaves

5 animals

5 balloons

Look out of the window.
Can you count 5 leaves?

6 six ● ● ●
● ● ●

6 arms

6 legs

6 whiskers

6 dates

Look around the room.
Can you count 6 legs?

7 seven

7 trees

7 pegs

7 flowers

Look out of the window.
Can you count 7 trees?

8   eight

8 flowerpots

8 mice

Can you squeak like a mouse?
Squeak 8 times!

9 nine

9 animals

9 stars

Wait until it gets dark.
Can you count 9 stars?

10 ten

10 fingers

10 toes

Look at your hands.
Can you count 10 fingers?

Wait until bathtime.
Look at your feet.
Can you count 10 toes?

Percy's Busy Day

One, two, what shall I do?

Three, four, out of the door

Five, six, pick up sticks

Seven, eight, it's getting late

Nine, ten, home again!